PUPPIES
Need Someone to Love

By P. Mignon Hinds

Illustrated by June Goldsborough

A GOLDEN BOOK • NEW YORK

Western Publishing Company, Inc., Racine, Wisconsin 53404

Text copyright © 1981 by Western Publishing Company, Inc. Illustrations copyright © 1981 by June Goldsborough. All rights reserved. Printed in the U.S.A. No part of this book may be reproduced or copied in any form without written permission from the publisher. GOLDEN®, GOLDEN & DESIGN®, A GOLDEN LOOK-LOOK® BOOK, and A GOLDEN BOOK® are trademarks of Western Publishing Company, Inc. Library of Congress Catalog Card Number: 80-84786 ISBN 0-307-11864-9/ISBN 0-307-61864-1 (lib. bdg.)   I J

Puppies are frisky, friendly, lovable baby animals.
They need many things to keep them happy and healthy.

Newborn puppies need
their mother's love and care.
    Puppies should stay with their mother
until they are six weeks old.

When puppies get older, they need a special place of their own.

Puppies can get very thirsty. They should have a bowl that is always filled with fresh water.

Puppies have little stomachs.
While puppies are growing they need
small meals several times each day.

Puppies' teeth grow, too.
Chewing helps a puppy's tiny teeth
to break through the gums.
Puppies need puppy toys
to chew on...

so they won't
chew on other things.

Sometimes puppies need a bath—
but not until they are six months old.

Puppies need to be brushed often
to keep their coats clean and shiny.

Puppies take lots of naps.
A sleepy puppy should have
a warm, cozy bed.

Puppies need a safe place
to run and play.

Sometimes puppies can get lost.
They should always wear a dog license
and name tag.

In cities and towns,
puppies should be on a leash
when they go for a walk.

Puppies need an animal doctor to give them checkups and take care of them when they are sick.

Puppies are smart.
They can learn to do tricks
and to come when they are called.

Mischievous puppies
need to be told when they are
doing something naughty.

Good puppies should be told
when they do the right thing.

A gentle hug is a good way of saying,
"You are the best puppy in the world."

Puppies need hugging.

Puppies need scolding.

Puppies need to eat
and sleep and play.

But most of all, puppies
need someone to love.